Feed My Sheep, They are Dying, Servant Leader is Needed

SHIRLEY A. YOUNG, ED.D

Uriel Press

Uriel Press books may be ordered through booksellers or by contacting:

Uriel Press
1663 Liberty Drive
Bloomington, IN 47403
www.urielpress.com
844-752-3114

ISBN: 979-8-8861-2013-4 (sc)
ISBN: 979-8-8861-2014-1 (e)

Library of Congress Control Number: 2022921615

Print information available on the last page.

Urial Press rev. date: 12/2/2022

CONTENTS

CHAPTER THREE

ACKNOWLEDGMENTS

My deepest gratitude goes to God for his provisions and spiritual encouragement to pursue doctoral studies, despite the struggles gave an obedient response, receiving rich knowledge.

Additionally, I want to thank the entire staff of Argosy University for their excellent assistance during my studies from 2012-2014 based in part on Drs. Tom Kemp and Anne Nelson for their tireless counsel and direction in encouraging and guiding me to succeed.

Finally thanks to my sons, extended family, clergy, ministry colleagues, and, friends for giving me much-needed support over the past 4 years of the journey.

DEDICATION

I dedicate my doctoral degree to my Lord and Savior Jesus Christ. It was His command and his presence that provided me the inspiration to fulfill my goal and succeed. God knew His servant's obedience with the ability to fulfill the assignment that would improve leaders in non-profit and profit organizations.

Additionally, I dedicate my work posthumously to my parents, James and Anna McNeely, who both inspired me, their eldest daughter to achieve a doctoral. Notably, my maternal grandmother, Hester Silver Jenkins Lamb, was an English professor whose example helped me aspire to my highest level of achievement. Additionally, throughout my educational journey, Iska Alter, Professor Emeriti of English at Hofstra University in Garden City, N.Y. encouraged me.

During my master's studies, I met Katie Geneva Cannon, Professor of Christian Ethics at Presbyterian School of Christian Education in Richmond, Virginia. Dr. Cannon's encouraging words "nothing is impossible with God" to persevere, was inspiring to attain this level of achievement.

Therefore, go and make disciples of all the nations, baptizing them in the name of the Father and the Son and the Holy Spirit. Teach these new disciples to obey all the commands I have given you. And be sure of this: I am with you always, even to the end of the age. (Matthew 28:19-20, NLT), Bible Gateway

Introduction

Christ's command spoken in Matthew 28 leaving the Great Commission to enhance the Kingdom of God reveals there is a decline in foundational Christian Education within Faith organizations that refutes discipleship growth. The 21st century presents the opportunity for senior clergy to assess whether Christian Education should be foundational or obsolete. Ecclesiastically, discipleship growth through Christian Education should be foundational for the body of believers to spiritually mature through teaching. Upon retiring in 1997 and transitioning in 1998 to Hampton, VA to continue my discipleship journey with a Faith-based organization (FBO), Christian Education was not seen to be foundationally strong for discipleship growth. Connection to an ecclesiastic and evangelical organization should give continuous discipleship growth. Additional concern became revelatory learning that clergy who formerly were Sunday school teachers were extending sermon messages into scheduled Sunday school hours refuting Sunday school teaching. Sunday school is a ministry that grows disciples of all ages.

> **Evangelical relates to the Christian gospel as told in the four gospels and ecclesiastical relates to the church and its functions.**

Being a lifetime Sunday school student growing through my spiritual journey became disheartened to learn that faith organizations are canceling Sunday school in the 21st century. The biblical verse of Matthew 28:19-20 commands that all disciples are to go and make more disciples, teaching them to obey all that God commands.

The text became continuously audible while hearing the voice of God saying, to pursue additional knowledge. Let children receive knowledge early: "People were bringing their children to Jesus to have him touch them, but the disciples rebuked them" (Mark 10:13 (NIV). This response was disturbing to Christ, as He wants children to come and be blessed by his WORD!! "Do not stop a child from seeking the knowledge of God" knowing God sent his son to give mankind another opportunity to have an everlasting relationship with Him after Adam caused mankind to fall, breaking our relationship with God.

21st -century leaders began exhibiting immoral and unethical behavioral attitudes affecting the integrity of FBOs leaders and not influencing the image of Christ to followers. Since transitioning from northern culture to southern culture, it is obvious there is a plummet in discipleship teaching which is disheartening.

Matthew 28:19-20 became extant during the research for leadership concern relative to Robert Greenleaf's 1970 study of a student's revolt versus university employees lacking character traits with incompetency. In preparation for the dissertation, the plethora of literature research data gave Greenleaf's study of ten character traits together with Kouzes and Posner leadership standards the resources that could transform today's leaders. This resource applies to profit and non-profits including faith-based organizations giving new leadership constructs. The research did accomplish a successful statistical analysis by having cooperative participants employ a leadership survey. Research results were enlightening in that FBOs require new leadership constructs to consider transformation through teaching and training. Again, Matthew 28:19-20 would continue to become visual and give clarity to the research theory, specifically the probability that leaders are not all "called" by God but appointed causing disparity in ministry. Senior clergy leaders are selecting secular leaders, not revering the spiritual "call" servants that could influence Christ.

Christian education for FBOs is obsolete failing to teach moral behaviors and attitudes. The foundation for the ecclesiastical order is Christian Educational knowledge for every believer according to Matthew 28:19-20 is by command of God.

I am reminded of Mike Slaughter saying: "*We have dumbed down what it means to be a disciple of Jesus Christ* (2014. p19)" and he also speaks of his cultural shock giving rise to writing, "The Renegade Christ". As God's servants, we cannot remain silent but allow God to use us to enlighten his disciples during this 21st century.

According to Matthew 28, it is the GREAT COMMISSION that mandates clergies to reach to teach for spiritual development and for faith-based organizations to maintain this command. This new resource introduces new constructs for educators, senior clergy, and ministry leaders to evaluate self and subordinate leaders for transformation. Transformation for leaders will introduce character traits of Christ the ultimate servant leader with an assessment of your spiritual influence on others.

The research gives knowledge that there is one type of leader, i.e. Servant leader deriving from the riot with students in a university as Greenleaf (1977) affirms this based on receiving unsavory service. This resource presents successful results allowing society an opportunity to teach and transform individuals from leaders to servants.

CHAPTER ONE

Purpose

It became enlightening after obeying God's command to research behaviors of leaders serving in profit and non-profit organizations finding invaluable references through an extensive literature review.

The problem was examined to learn that the values and actions of leaders in faith-based organizations (FBOs) are being compromised, resulting in a loss of integrity, trust, and confidence in leaders, lacking success within the organization with disruption of the leader's gifts. In a study regarding the clerical abuse crisis in the United States, it was learned that McGrath-Merkle (2010) noted that Roman Catholic bishops in the United States were being protected in abuse cases while the children involved were not protected.

McGrath-Merkle (2010) posed the question, "Why did religious leaders protect the criminals and not protect the children?" Statistics indicated that 53.3% of offending bishops were sent for psychological treatment, 7% were sent on spiritual retreats, 6.1% were removed from their positions, 2.6% had no action taken against them, and 9% were reprimanded and returned to active ministry. McGrath-Merkle (2010) purported an impropriety is levied; a leader loses his or her leadership influence quality, which can result in the annihilation of others and the world at large. McGrath-Merkle (2010) pursued a psychological research study with Freud and Erikson to answer his question. Peus, Wesche, Streicher, Braun, and Frey (2012) noted similar problems with similar results—offending leaders were protected. Seidel (2003) noted leadership problems regarding values and actions involved flaws, cracks, and limitations of a leader's character.

The goal of the study was to compare Greenleaf's (2008) servant leader theory with two other theories to develop a new set of guidelines that could be used to assist leaders of FBO in regaining high values and developing appropriate actions. Additionally, the goal was to increase the success and growth of FBO organizations based on leaders emulating the character traits of a servant leader, combined with the ethical values and appropriate leadership styles proposed by other theorists.

The results of the study were expected to be important based on the social and economic influence of nonprofit organizations in the United States. Sarantopoulos (2008) reported that the nonprofit business sector in the United States is among the largest worldwide, employing over 1.6 million employees and controlling $2.4 trillion in assets. Therefore, the values and actions of FBO leaders can influence society positively or negatively overall.

Society should be aware that relationships are a paramount issue in successful leadership, i.e., Avolio, Walumbwa, and Weber (2009) examined relationships between leaders and followers to provide goals for developing strategies to change and improve leaders. Avolio et al. (2009) showed using servant leader traits can be used to improve FBOs and leaders in the 21st century. Peus et al. (2012) suggested that the values of leaders are collapsing, resulting in a loss of integrity, trust, and confidence from followers.

Further, Schyns and Schilling (2013) explored the most effective methods used to find leaders who lead by focusing on positive leadership behaviors. Schyns and Schilling (2013) believed destructive leadership behaviors exist within organizations. Based on statistics gathered in the Netherlands, Schyns and Schilling (2013) showed 11% of destructive leadership behaviors within organizations, with higher rates in the Norwegian study and 13.6% in the United States.

Schyns and Schilling (2013) showed the severe effects that destructive leadership behaviors had on followers. Vondey (2012) asserted that the characteristics of an effective leader create similar characteristics in followers. Therefore, for followers to show integrity/honesty and assumption of responsibility, their leaders must exhibit the same characteristics. A Gallup poll indicated that a mere 22% of Americans trust business leaders, while fewer Americans trust political leaders (Darvish & Rezaei, 2011). Darvish and Rezaei (2011) indicated the statistics present a potential disaster, not merely a problem in leadership. The Gallup survey has been useful in supporting researchers who proposed requiring modes to improve leadership for the 21st century. Darvish and Rezaei (2011) showed that over the last 100 years, researchers in the leadership field have provided valuable knowledge about leadership to improve the field. Retrieving resource data introduces new constructs to improve leadership performances. Reed, Vidaver-Cohen, and Colwell (2011) addressed recent scandals within the sectors of business, government, sports, nonprofits, and other institutions and raised questions regarding the quality of organizational leadership.

Seidel (2003) provided a list of characteristic failures/flaws that leaders have exhibited. The failures/flaws include (a) the need to be right, (b) the desire to be in control, (c) the inordinate need for attention involving approval and appreciation, and (d) traits of neediness (Seidel, 2003). Seidel (2003) introduced traits and feelings among leaders who have experienced failures including the following feelings: (a) they never did enough, (b) they were never good, (c) they used others for personal gain, (d) they were unwilling to take risks, (e) they feared rejection, (f) the inability to take a stance on an issue, and (g) they were divisive.

Antonakis, Ashkanasy, and Dasborough (2009) found the making of good leaders depends on their intelligence and the willingness to identify their weaknesses in communicating their vision.

Additionally, Antonakis et al. (2009) stated leaders should have personality characteristics that permit them to mobilize their followers. Smith (2005) indicated Greenleaf entitled his work "Servant as Leader" and not "Leader as Servant" purposefully. Greenleaf (2008) used his original 1970 theory of the *servant as leader* or *servant leadership* as his method to seek a descriptor that could provoke leaders to cogitate on the proposed challenge and theory. Greenleaf (2008) perceived combining the two contradictory terms as a method to create reflection on leadership theory. Greenleaf (2008) proposed long-standing assumptions of possessive relationships between leaders and followers. Additionally, Greenleaf (2008) was aware of the historically negative connotation of the word *servant*; therefore, he believed it was necessary to move quickly into a new view of leadership by creating a new paradigm. Smith (2005) found that Greenleaf embraced the two contradictory terms of servant and leader in *The Servant as Leader* to create change. Smith (2005) suggested that Greenleaf did not invert the terms to read "the leader as a servant" so that the new paradigm would be created with contradictory terms.

Fry (2003) desired to create change for leaders, taking note of the accelerated call for spirituality. Fry (2003) described the universal human need for calling and membership for spiritual survival. Meanwhile, Greenleaf (2008) developed the definition of a servant leader as a new leadership model to identify the specific characteristics or attributes of a servant leader. Greenleaf indicated a difference exists between the leader's role of servant-first and the leader's role of leader-first.

Greenleaf (2008) provided 10 attributes or characteristic traits for servant leadership.

In the origins of servant leadership, Greenleaf (1977) showed a true indication of concern for researchers to identify successful leadership characteristic traits to implement among 21st-century leaders.

In 1960, Greenleaf attempted to comprehend why many young people were rebelling against institutions in America, specifically within universities (Greenleaf, 1977, p. 28). Greenleaf (2008) used his insight into the rebellion of young people against the institutions to conclude that behaviors were indicators of poor serving and leader standards. Hoveida and Salari (2011) supported Greenleaf's original writing of the student's dissatisfaction with servants in the institutes. Seidel (2003) stated leaders' flaws and rebellion by youth showed a fault that represented a "crack" in leadership, affirming that leaders were lacking in serving, leading skills, and attitudes. Greenleaf was inspired to write an essay in 1972 entitled, *"The Institution as Servant"*. Greenleaf's (2009) essay focused on institutions being universities, churches, hospitals, and organizations to teach character traits of being "servant leaders". In his essay, Greenleaf (2009) conveyed hope despite his observation of a massive failure among leaders in many educational institutions in America. Greenleaf (2009) began to affirm leaders were Servants, trustees were servants, clergies were servants and teachers were servants in every aspect of their performance. Greenleaf became aware that employment in the mentioned positions gave knowledge that individuals are serving others needing character traits.

In her study of Greenleaf, Smith (2005) identified four central tenets regarding the servant leadership framework. Greenleaf's tenets had the following goals: (a) leaders needed to be true to self when serving others, (b) leaders needed to have a holistic approach for success to rethink relationships with others and with organizations, and (c) leaders needed to promote a sense of community among followers, and (d) leaders needed to enable others to act through empowering using collective decision-making and elimination of hoarding power (as cited by Smith, 2005).

Smith (2005) referenced other theorists who developed lists of attributes with similar traits to Greenleaf. Smith (2005) referenced Russell and Stone (2002) who proposed a list of 20 attributes for servant leadership. Joseph and Winston (2005) presented honesty, integrity, and benevolence as a few attributes of servant leaders. Smith (2005) identified other theorists who developed attributes including Sendjaya and Sarros (2002), and Smith, Montagno, and Kuzmenko (2004).

Chu (2011) asserted Greenleaf's theory presented two questions for servant leaders. First, can a servant leader become passive and avoid conflicts? Second, do servant leaders have the natural propensity to handle conflicts using compromise or obligatory natural styles for serving others (Chu 2011)? Further, Chu (2011) stated that not all conflicts are negative.

Patterson (2003) provided a theoretical model of servant leadership constructs that worked together to commence with love and conclude with service. Patterson (2003) theorized that the servant leader is a role model in behavior and styles, showing others within an organization how to serve and set a climate. In a review of Patterson's theory, Dennis (2004) identified limitations and began an extensive study using experts to investigate an understanding of leadership constructs.

Dennis (2004) replicated the leadership style and behavioral constructs of Patterson (2003) by requiring an instrument for measuring servant leadership. Dennis (2004) used a sample of participants with random sampling but did not test with self-assessment for servant leadership [e.g., LPIS] (Kouzes & Posner, 2013). Therefore, Dennis (2004) recommended that other researchers consider a self-assessment instrument to test leaders.

Author's 21ˢᵗ Century View for Leadership

Since the initial publication, I became aware leaders are displaying behaviors and attitudes becoming demonstrable affecting relationships with their subordinates. The concern is occurring within the profit and nonprofit organizations reaching the level of our nation's leaders i.e. Presidents, senators, government officials, CEOs, subordinates, Clergy, and hierarchal order i.e. Popes, Bishops, and Priests. Thereby influencing the loss of reputation, and integrity, marring the character of individuals who were once honored with high esteem.

The research study being successful gives a

resource tool of LPI that assesses individuals who are willing to commit to an evaluation. It will assess their character traits as "servant leaders" and not just a leader. The definition of "servant leader" activates a difference in performance, as there are traits that complement their daily actions. It is these traits that define the difference between a leader and a servant leader. The evaluation will indicate weaknesses and/or strengths depending on the individual's performance over time before the assessment.

If there are weak traits, then teaching would be required using the resources available to give individuals strength to improve their "servant leader" performance.

The objective is to transform individuals to "servant leadership" status and not "just a leader".

It is this author's aspiration that the reading audience would find this resource invaluable to become a "servant leader" willing to assess and transform to influence others with a reputable image for the 21st century.

Although the research study used demographics from faith-based leadership receiving a successful conclusion, the resource is also applicable to for-profit organizations including our government officials. The objective is to utilize this resource as a teaching tool to annually assess a leader's proficient performance with their character traits.

I would like the reading audience to do a self-examination of their serving role as an employee whether it is profit, nonprofit, or self-employment. Each individual should represent character traits that will make a difference in relationships and communication, with others. In addition, desire to attain their potential with proficiency as servant leaders.

During the pandemic that began in March 2020 through December 2021, I had six-week virtual sessions teaching, "Leader to Servant leader" to individuals interested in enhancing their character within their job or church, using the LPI assessment. This is a re-edited publication for for-profit and non-profit organizations to transform leaders into "Servant Leaders".

Christian Education
is Foundational

According to the biblical text of Matthew 28:19 teaching is a command by Christ and shepherds should structure foundational teaching through Christian Education Ministry to develop discipleship growth for all ages. Remember, Christ gave the Great Commission to go and teach, as this is a continuous and eternal assignment to reach disciples to the far corners of the world. Each disciple requires training to benefit knowledge to teach other disciples so that all will follow and obey the biblical command.

As an obedient servant, I gave response to

God's request to pursue a research study for servant leadership benefitting knowledge that the image of Christ is lost requiring restoration. It affirms the gratification of obedience to an assignment that was unclear believing irrelevant to becoming relevant for-profit and nonprofit organizations. The relevancy introduces Robert Greenleaf's (2008) ten character traits to transform faith-based organizations (FBOs) leadership universally.

> *In those days, I will pour out my Spirit, even on my servants—men and women alike – and they will prophesy. Acts 2:18 (NLT) Bible Gateway*

This word encourages all servants that God will pour out his spirit and they will "*prophesy*" is one of several gifts God gives to his disciples. Disciples benefit from knowledge through Christian Education when it is foundationally structured and perpetually active within FBOs. In this 21st century, there are so many social issues causing families to be broken, and losing children at an early age. To escape false teaching, the FBOs should have foundational Christian Education to give strength to servants weak in faith and worship experience. Why choose and accept a lifestyle and not teach you knowledge about the lifestyle? FBOs should have this answer well established.

> *Now the Holy Spirit tells us clearly that in the last times some will turn away from what we believe; they will follow lying spirits and teachings that come from demons. These teachers are hypocrites and liars. They pretend to be religious, but their consciences are dead. 1 Timothy 4:1-2 (NLT) Bible Gateway*

> *If you keep yourself pure, you will be a special utensil for honorable use. Your life will be clean, and you will be ready for the Master to use you for every good work. 2 Timothy 2:21 (NLT) Bible Gateway*

Timothy affirms what can be possible if teaching is available through Christian Education for disciples to mature as servant-leader for the glory of God. Everyone is not going to be submissive and obedient to the Word of God, but make it possible for as many to accept Christ and follow his command. As the author of this writing, Christian Education has been my foundation since the early age of 2. I have been blessed to have had this foundation throughout my years to now share globally the stronghold it gives in growing a close relationship with God. **The more we learn about God, the more we grow closer to God and the stronger our relationship becomes with HIM!**

> *Now, these are the gifts Christ gave to the church, the apostles, the prophets, the evangelists, and the pastors and teachers. Ephesians 4:11 (NLT) Bible Gateway*

FBOs must structure Christian Education perpetually, as there are many believers lacking knowledge of having a God-given gift. "Spiritual Gifts" "You are a Masterpiece" or "Gift or Talent trap" are classes unknown to many. Many individuals have experienced weekly worship for over thirty or more years lacking knowledge of having a specific assignment given by God to fulfill His Will for their life. Many believers are unaware that Christ is the "Ultimate Servant Leader" and "Teacher" with many shepherds always wanting to "Preach" than "teach" and have "facilitators" instead of having "teachers". Hosea 4:6 reminds us that we perish for lack of knowledge.

FBOs with established Christian Education are few and far between for believers to benefit from perpetual teaching for discipleship growth. My foundation of biblical learning was in New York City with FBOs in each of our five boroughs giving the availability of free teaching sessions weekly. Individuals were required to register, commit and complete the free assignments. Our time does not belong to any one of us and therefore having the privilege to receive free learning meant giving time for the benefit of knowledge. After retiring from New York and transitioning to the southern culture, I am experiencing a continuous culture shock. Only a few and far between churches have Christian Education perpetually structured that reflects shepherds are not obeying **THE GREAT COMMISSION.**

What is most important is to have teaching structured from infancy to 100 in the FBOs, as was my experience in the northern culture that is not seen in the southern culture. Yet, many leaders transitioned from the North to the South and did not introduce their experience. What is more reflective is when disciples take membership at another FBO they are unable to integrate their spiritual growth/gifting within the ministry. Shepherds today appear not to have spiritual discernment to know that God sends servants to serve the vision that He gives to fulfill his will.

As I have said, the body of believers has an age range, which indicates, that teaching must be applicable for infants when they come with their parents. This age group began my teaching experience after being prepared and trained for my gifting of teaching. I teach, you can process your gifting after hearing the voice of God speak such as I experienced. *God's voice was clear when he said, "Teach my people". I was startled, remained quiet, and the words were spoken for a second time. I accepted the command and the next day phoned the church office asking for an appointment with the pastor. It amazed me how I was processed by my pastor.*

He immediately began writing and handed me a list of classes to take at Abyssinia B.C. Bible institute as well as classes at our Bible institute and then to teach his class to fulfill the preparation. I did not have a financial obligation but to set time with a commitment to fulfill this requirement. I obediently accomplished the process and met it with excellence receiving my first assignment to teach infants. It was a profound experience speaking the Word of God, singing songs, and planting the spirit of God in the minds and hearts of the innocent.

Christian Education tracks the life of sheep and/or of a disciple, what a disciple is to do, why they must do it, and know their purpose for God as they journey with the Holy Spirit taking charge of their life. When FBOs have Christian Education foundationally structured, it develops and grows disciples into a relationship with God to receive all that he promises and to know they are servant-leaders with gifting. Christ, the ultimate servant leader, gives each disciple an assignment to image Him and become a servant leader. Additionally, Christian Education enhances the growth of each disciple with the constitution and by-laws of their organization's faith to prevent false doctrine and teach Biblical doctrine.

The church cannot overlook infancy, toddlers, adolescent, teens, young adults, adults, and elders. Take note of the stages of maturity for humans, the same is for lambs to sheep. There are faith-based organizations (FBOs) that are bypassing the young age and young adults to have only elders. Why? 21st-century parents' method is to let children stay home believing they must mature and understand the purpose to attend worship. Some parents believe when their children finish high school they can better comprehend the worship experience. Many parents lack knowledge that the Word speaks to the infant and cannot bypass the aging process by jumping to the older age.

Life tracks our behavior, mind, heart, love, and, respect from the first day of life until God gives us our final rest. *Give thought to a shepherd caring for their flock, the lamb growing into maturity to become a sheep being nurtured by a shepherd. If we were to slaughter lambs, there will be no sheep to mature and the mature sheep would be extinct.* This is an example of a church without children and only the elders.

Christian Education teaches disciples about evangelism, missions, ushering, and other areas of ministry to use their gifting. As it is said disciples must grow to have a closer relationship with God.

What's most profound is that many disciples are unaware when they attend weekly worship they are going to a hospital to receive healing. Each week conditions develop needing treatment and many disciples are unaware the church is their healing station. Healing requires doses of special treatment that come through weekly messages along with teaching that also gives healing. There is an answer for every believer who is an intent listener, taking notes for their weekly healing.

CHAPTER TWO

Types of Leaders

As leaders serve in this 21st century, there are different types of leaders serving in various genres of employment in profit or non-profit entities. The research was quite enlightening with findings being informative and reflecting different types of leaders specifically "servants". As stated earlier in the writing, the two authors, Robert Greenleaf and Kouzes & Posner became the foundation for the research study. Their works complemented my research to conclude with a Fact and negated the theory giving successful results.

I am grateful for obeying God's voice to research leadership behaviors benefitting knowledge that faith organizations are refuting perpetual and foundational Christian Education. If there is structure and perpetual availability for knowledge, disciples will grow to know they are to image and model Christ to influence others to become "servant leaders".

UNCALLED VS CALLED LEADERS

There are many "uncalled" shepherds in faith organizations unaware of knowing that God chooses a "Called" leader. "Uncalled" shepherds become the overseer of the "uncalled" they chose for servant leaders. Unfortunately, the "Uncalled" does not serve until their pastor gives orders that determine "when and what". The "Uncalled" are those like "Saul", and individuals selected by clergy to be a diaconate or to be ordained to preach lacking clear knowledge of their assignment and are managed by the clergy who appointed them. There is a difference between "Called" and "Uncalled" leaders specifically in the faith organizations than in profit and/or other non-profit organizations.

In the faith-based, "Called" are spirit-directed, spirit-led, and spirit-filled individuals receiving an assignment i.e. "Abram", "Joshua", and "Isaiah" to name a few. There is a spiritual anointing upon the "called" that the "uncalled" does not receive. The "called" has an aura of God's spiritual presence when God chooses His servant leaders with an assignment. Abram did hear God when God said to leave your country and go where I direct you. He obediently responded without question (Genesis 12:1-5 - (NIV). God told Joshua that He will be with him as He was with Moses (Joshua 1:5). Joshua had the assurance of knowing that God is with those He chooses and will direct them with their assignment and will not leave or forsake them keeping His promise. Romans 1:1 God called Paul to be an apostle, set apart for the Gospel of God. Romans 8:28 – We know that in all things God works for the good of those who love him, who have been called according to his purpose.

This writer recollects senior pastors were "called" with a gift of spiritual discernment imaging the characteristics of Christ the ultimate "servant leader". The "called" leader having spiritual discernment knows Christian educational teaching is mandatory to comprehend the command to a "call". When God calls you and you inform your pastor who should then send you (the disciple) for training to obediently respond and be equipped for the assignment. When a constituent connects to a new faith organization, the senior pastor lacking spiritual discernment and having no active Christian Education, make it impossible to process the new individual with their gifting to continue discipleship growth.

The "Called" serves to obey God's directives and in some cases will cease only if their pastor becomes intimidated should their performance not please him.

Through my experience, the senior pastor would say, "keep on doing what you are doing", which gave confirmation we should be "Called" leaders and not "Uncalled-leader". It is compelling to negate knowing you are to obey what God has assigned you to do. Disciples must learn to know when God speaks directly to them (His chosen ones) serve obediently according to his WILL to receive his blessings. When disciples find quiet time to meditate, they will hear the soft voice of God giving them directives, especially in John 21:16 affirming to the disciples what Christ commands. Every disciple receives an assignment from God through his son Jesus Christ. There is anticipation that disciples shall fulfill their gifting according to the Will of God and not cast it aside as obsolete.

Disciples that are "called" might experience family members speaking negative remarks about their anointing. They will observe that you are different and will not embrace you but display hatred towards you. It is your faith and commitment that will take control during these trials to determine who you are in Christ. You will experience similar actions as Christ did as you obey the voice of God to serve his people.

GENERAL LEADERSHIP

General leadership has been a subject of intense study throughout the 21st century. While the concepts of general leadership theory are used to guide leaders to influence their followers, general leadership theories do not provide specific leadership traits as servant leadership will define.

A researcher expressed a phenomenal remark about leaders and leadership stating leaders are comparable to an artist with their intuitiveness and creativity in the performance of their work. The reference of being comparable to an artist became pervasive in teaching spiritual gifting to inform a leader of their purpose.

The uniqueness of each believer being a masterpiece of art soon develops an identity and builds self-esteem giving strength and capability to serve God.

There is the recollection of a Sunday school lesson on "Creation" at the early age of thirteen experiencing low self-esteem, sad about life, and learning that God's love uniquely designed me, and gave new beginnings to my life overcoming the past. This gives rise to why Christian education is vital for thousands of ages 0 to 100 broken within, requiring resolution of their pain and past hurts for healing and renewal.

The 21st century is identifying leaders and leadership qualities that are rising and falling without defining any determining qualities once they benefit knowledge of having a gift from God.

Research data indicates leadership needs new constructs to develop literature for organizational behaviors with media circulating unethical and immoral issues of leaders serving ecclesiastically and in corporate America. Leaders take risks in their role that is essential for organizational followership making decisions to satisfy their commitment to grow people and the organization. "Servant leader" and not just general leader is a new focus recognizing that a servant influences relationships having the intent to grow an organization and transform for the good of society with a multidirectional performance between their role and followers.

SPIRITUAL LEADERSHIP

FBO leaders with the title of spiritual leader assimilate their role with no specific performance and is different from servant leaders with clergy appointing and micromanaging. The spiritual leader verbally exercises the Holy writ publically demonstrating the appearance of being set apart from others and having sanctification. Clergy refuting Christian pedagogy hampers disciples' maturity to attain clergy micromanaging leaders and spiritual leaders. The research study of organizational leadership became informative being unaware of different types of leaders. Introducing this resource awakens knowledge to consider transforming faith-based leaders globally.

Sanders (2003) asserted God develops spiritual leaders within faith organizations and God gives directions for spiritual leaders to serve. Additionally, Sanders (2003) stated a genuine leader focuses on serving God and others without coaxing.

Fry (2003) noted that Greenleaf's servant leadership theory provided a holistic approach for leaders that outlined the full needs and approaches essential for leaders and followers. Spiritual leadership is comprised of three theories of vision: altruistic love, hope, and faith. She concludes that spiritual leaders respond to the call of holistic leadership that involves the integration of the mind, body, heart, and spirit.

SERVANT LEADERSHIP

Servant Leadership is a phrase coined by Robert Greenleaf in his work, "The Servant Leader", published in 1970 and revised in 2008. Researchers since 1970 have been broadening Greenleaf's concept by informing people about "servant and not leader" character traits.

When God chooses his servants, they should not ignore but should obey his voice. Unfortunately, many fail to inquire as Samuel did when he heard God speak to him and obeyed his command to serve. We can reject man, but be careful when you say, "No" to God's command.

The entitlement of "Servant leader" is new to leaders of faith organizations, as Christ is the ultimate servant leader for disciples to exemplify as believers. The essence of servant leaders is they serve selflessly and selfishly, as leaders lack understanding of being a servant first and a leader second. An additional viewpoint to recognize is that Greenleaf's study views servant leaders following a calling to serve others by responding to ethics and abiding laws of God. Let individuals know they will become servants while maturing using the new character traits and behaviors.

The fact that other researchers were acknowledging additional paradigms supports the affirmation of needing transformation in the 21st century for FBOs. Research indicates in recent years there have been media and press releases about leadership behaviors with a need to address, assess and determine organizational authenticity.

In addition, the thought to consider leadership authenticity comparable to God's authenticity of "calling" will not have "leaders selected" but to consider qualification. Authenticity would be visible when disciples receive teaching, and training to image Christ to other disciples and share the word to enhance their growth.

The growth and development through the word have similarities to infant birth to maturity of adulthood and how disciples receive teaching with comprehension of the Word of God benefitting its truths. There is the opportunity for disciples to take an assessment of their spiritual growth that determines the level of maturity available using the LPI assessment.

Research recommends there is a need to assess authentic leadership constructs that might be unique and contribute to positive results to transform leaders into servant leaders. There is contention through researching "servant leadership" that leaders with visions can implement their visions and define the direction of an organization. Notably, the "servant leader" concept is essential in profit organizations as they are servants first desiring to help people become successful, responding to the needs and interests of others with aspiration. Greenleaf who was a clergy introduces the servant leader concept as a derivative of the foundational teaching of Jesus Christ and biblical accounts and not an original idea. This knowledge gives rise to transforming staff into servant leaders in for-profit and non-profit organizations. This is a recommendation since the budgets of organizations are depleted and unable to give perpetual annual training for staff workers to be proficient servants.

Currently, faith followers face challenges of ineffective leadership lacking comprehension of Christ having character traits requiring continuous teaching that will give foundation to the faith organizations.

When the performance of a leader is authentic, it prevents global societal indifferences within organizations. The goal of the resource is to define and compare leaders with servant leaders.

The research data on character traits is to provide in-depth insight to improve the abilities and effectiveness of leaders in faith organizations. Christ the ultimate servant leader gives an image for leaders universally. After Greenleaf's 1972 study of his first essay created the term "Servant Leader", the establishment of the Greenleaf Leadership Center in Westfield, Indiana continues to revise editions of Greenleaf's work of additional concepts for servant leadership.

As an obedient servant, I gave a response to God's request to pursue a research study for servant leadership benefitting knowledge that the image of Christ is lost requiring restoration of Christian Education in faith-based organizations (FBOs). It affirms the gratification of obedience to an assignment that was unclear believing irrelevant to becoming relevant for-profit and nonprofit organizations. The relevancy introduces Robert Greenleaf's (2008) ten character traits to transform organizational leaders globally. Additionally, with Kouzes & Posner's (2004) five standards of leadership to embrace Servant Leaders as Christ our ultimate servant leader.

Profit and Faith-Based Organizations

The profit organizations did give annual sessions to improve their staff workers' behaviors and character traits for efficient performance to uphold the integrity of the organization. These sessions were beneficial for the retention of employees. Employees during the 20th century were fortunate to work for organizations

We are in the 21st century losing innumerable children, youth, and, teens. There is the remembrance of my 20th-century days as a youth living in NYC experiencing gangs, shoot-outs, bullying, and the loss of many young lives. You would say "hello" in the a.m. and they would be gone by dinnertime. You would speak to a mother today and by the weekend, she has been shot and killed. The question then and still speaks in this dispensation: where is the CHURCH during the upheaval and losses?

Is the church meant to transform lives, enrich life, give hope for happiness and joy, or neglect service to the community losing one another daily by abuse, neglect, and poverty? When people lack knowledge, they perish!!! This appears to be quite vivid in society today through media, communities, and voices. The leaders of a church are asking, "Where are the people?" but not asking, "Where are the children"? It was in Hampton, VA 2007 at Hampton University when Radio Host Tavis Smiley hosted a celebration for "Jamestown 400th Anniversary", raising the question, "Where are the Babies"? That was the first and last time this question was raised having prominent speakers i.e. clergy, attorneys, professors, and others. Yet, death is prevalent daily and globally as we observe the innumerable children and youth that are out of control.

My question is: Where are the faith-based organizational leaders and where is the parental discipline? There was a time when parents and the church were operating together giving strongholds for children's future. It now appears that the stronghold has fallen through the cracks and children are at loose ends.

The schools are losing their purpose revealing the need to improve leadership.

I am a product of a church growing 350 children, youth, and teens in NYC in gangland territory with parents saying, "You must go to church" having no choice. The church foundationally had classes during the week as well as on Saturdays and Sundays for children and youth teaching the knowledge of Christ. There were sessions on Saturdays to enlighten the youth of the antichrist that was a daily struggle within the communities, needing to know how to negate and accept Christ.

Unfortunately, faith organizations are not organized to adequately serve children, adolescents, and teens together with family members in this 21st century. Obeying God's voice in 2009 gives credence to the results of my leadership research. Additionally, Matthews 28:19-20 fully supports the current status of faith organizations' disobedience to God's Command, to GO and TEACH.

Comparison of
General Leadership to
Spiritual Leadership

This resource introduces new paradigms for for-profit and non-profit organizations to transform leaders to serve with excellence and proficiency. There are a plethora of general and spiritual leadership research studies that give further consideration to compare leadership performance. Many individuals serve for many years comfortably as a leader, lacking the knowledge they were more than just a leader. In the 20th century, questions would arise during my disciple journey about leadership performance.

It is now the 21st century that behaviors are affecting subordinates causing many to leave profit and non-profit organizations. Globally during this 21st century, it is important to enlighten the hierarchal of organizations, there are new constructs to improve the behaviors and attitudes of organizational leaders.

It is learned there are general leaders, and spiritual leaders, and unaware there should be only one type of leader. The research study affirms the fact there should be "servant leaders" and not leaders, especially general or spiritual leaders.

Greenleaf affirms at the time of the student revolt the hired employees were serving in various capacities lacking characteristic traits while serving students and staff.

It is also notable that a general leader is different from a spiritual leader's performance in their behaviors, and character traits. It is important how general or spiritual leaders influence others as they carry out their assignments.

Within the body of congregants, many individuals are serving in ministries at different levels of spiritual growth that will determine the strength of their leadership influence. A general leader as opposed to a spiritual leader will bring a role of the generality of life having no faith connections. This affirms there is a difference between a general leader and a spiritual leader that is not based on their knowledge to lead a group.

Although, there are no specific traits for general leaders, they are appointed as willing workers, respectful, and dependable. They will falter along the way to resign after influencing unethical behavior.

Blackaby & Blackaby, (2011) did a study giving spiritual leader's pitfalls and influences i.e.: preparation, power, personality, God's hand, integrity, Successful record accomplishment, courage and humility vs Pitfalls i.e.: pride, spiritual lethargy, oversensitivity, administrative carelessness, prolong position holding, greed, domestic neglect and mental laziness. Please take note that Blackaby and Blackaby (2011) spiritual leadership influences and pitfalls are different from Robert Greenleaf (2005).

Additionally, Sanders (2003) gives several character traits of positive and perilous qualities. A few of Sanders (2003) Positive qualities: discipline, vision, wisdom, decision, courage, humility, integrity, humor, patience, friendship, listening; these are a few of Perilous qualities: egotism, pride, infallibility, jealousy, popularity, indispensability, depression, secular, greed, spiritual lethargy, mental laziness, competiveness and prolong position holding.

It is the research results that present the opportunity to introduce transformation in this 21st century for organizational leaders to improve ethically and morally. Ethical and moral behaviors are the purpose of doing the research study with leaders exhibiting unfavorable behaviors since the 20th century.

God's command to research behaviors of leaders in profit and non-profit organizations was a challenge to obey as it gave understanding for its purpose. At the inception of this research study, social media were exhibiting immoral and unethical behaviors in the workplace with high-profile leaders giving credence to pursue and fulfill this command with obedience.

It became knowledgeable that a myriad of authors did implicate types of leaders with intense research was able to receive fact and not an assumption that there is only one type of leader. The study met with expectations giving knowledge other authors were researching leadership character, although, nothing similar to Robert Greenleaf's study of

1977. (Sanders, (2003) lists different character traits that refers to spiritual leaders' positive and perilous qualities giving insight that leadership character traits have been influencing others over the years.

There a need for universal transformation from top-down in administrative organizational leadership for profit and non-profit organizations. It became further knowledgeable that as individuals, each one of us is a "servant" as we serve one another daily.

Comparison of Spiritual Leadership to Servant Leadership

The research results give the fact that there is one type of leader after comparing general to spiritual and spiritual to servant leadership. Yes, you can be a leader with different behaviors and attitudes that will require training and development to become an effective leader. Take note that a leader is a "servant" serving constituents in different capacities being capable of satisfying their assignment while influencing either a good or a bad image.

Comparing spiritual leaders to servant leaders is dependent upon the strengths of their character traits as they perform daily that recommend transforming to have the strong image of Christ.

Yes, there are spiritual leaders exercising character traits flaring unethically and immorally through the ecclesiastic order of worship affecting laymen and subordinates. Based on data through social media, the results of the research are a timely resource for 21st-century profit and non-profit organizations to globally consider transforming the character of leaders.

In all leadership types as discussed from the results of the research study, it is a fact that there are different behaviors with pitfalls that are extremely different from servant leadership.

The traits of spiritual and servant leaders are different in that servant leaders should be the dominant type of leader that Robert Greenleaf originally coined based on a student riot that broke out in 1977 at a Pennsylvania college. There is an LPI to be utilized by individuals desiring to know the weaknesses and strengths of their current character traits. This resource asks that individuals take the LPI assessment to begin their transformation into a "Servant Leader" recognizing there is only one true leader that should be performing globally making a societal difference. The LPI Assessment is found in the Appendix.

After discussing Spiritual leader influences and pitfalls of Blackaby & Blackaby (2011), taking note of positive and perilous qualities of Sanders (2003) reflects differences to Servant Leader performance. The research of character traits and practical behaviors of Greenleaf (2005) and Kouzes & Posner (2004) are compatible to the character of the Ultimate Servant Leader. These traits are what leaders have been influencing unethically and immorally in their behaviors and tolerated for decades.

Greenleaf (2005) gives ten character traits for a servant leader to influence Servant Leadership in their daily performance. These traits are: Awareness, Building community, Commitment, Conceptualization, Empathy, Foresight, Healing, Listening, Persuasion and Stewardship. Kouzes & Posner (2004) did a research for servant leaders giving Five Practices: Model the way; inspire a shared vision; Challenge the process, Enable others to act; and Encourage the heart. A servant leader using these five practices will give commitment to their act of behavior by finding their voice setting an example; envision the future and enlist others, search for opportunities and experiment by risk-taking, foster collaboration and strengthen others, recognize contributions, celebrate the values and victories.

Additionally, an assessment is recommended to evaluate leaders. The evaluation will give data that would indicate the weakness and strengths of a leader's level of maturity. The data gives the opportunity to further develop character and behavior practices by committing to a six-week teaching sessions to benefit 10 character traits and 5 practices to become a Servant Leader that will image Christ.

The success for this research became the ten traits for transforming into a servant leader. The leadership experience for this author began in my youth enhancing into adulthood. During these years, there were observations of leaders struggling with relationships and disrespect with subordinates not following governing plans and finding members inactive. At conferences or workshops, this would be a concerned problem for leaders within organizations. It was thought that individuals were psychologically afflicting others with their trauma. But this assumption was thwarted by learning it is more about types of leaders influencing character traits. The research satisfied giving fact and not an assumption using Greenleaf; Kouzes and Posner's studies having the solution of leaders needing transformation into servant leaders.

CHAPTER THREE

Conclusion

It was by divine order with an obedient response of this author and servant to research leadership behaviors as God commanded. The research gave a plethora of data that was able to successfully resolve assumptions into a fact of truth to enhance society for the 21st century.

Before analyzing the research results, the assumption was FBO leaders were ineffective with their followers. Using the survey to assess the identified problem (assumption) introduced an LPI-S instrument that is an invaluable tool to determine if leaders are servants, leaders, or effective leaders. Greenleaf (2008) indicated that his identified 10 character traits would be found in leaders who exemplify and emulate Christ, thus introducing new behaviors for servant leaders. Using the LPI-S instrument by Kouzes and Posner (2013b), the current study results provided a method to integrate the 10 traits with the 5 leadership practices to improve leader behaviors.

It is recommended that other researchers pursue organizational leadership transformation and conduct studies with more than 100 participants. Additional recommendations include seeking ethnicities of Korean, Pacific Islander, and Native–Americans within the denominations of Catholicism, Seventh Day Adventist, The Church of Jesus Christ of Latter-Day Saints, and Presbyterian. Organizational leadership is an exigent field; therefore, endeavors must exist to develop leadership foundations involving integrity and honesty.

BIBLIOGRAPHY

Antonakis, J., Ashkanasy, N. M., & Dasborough, M. T. (2009). Does leadership need emotional intelligence? *The Leadership Quarterly*, 20, 247-261. doi:10.1016/j.leaqua.2009.01.006

Avolio, B. J., Walumbwa, F. O., & Weber, T. J. (2009). Leadership: Current theories, research, and future directions. *Annual Review of Psychology*, 60, 421-449.

Blackaby, H., & Blackaby, R. (2011). *Spiritual leadership*. Nashville, TN: B & H.

Chu, R. I. (2011). *Conflict management styles of pastors and organizational servant leadership: A descriptive study* (Doctoral dissertation).

Available from ProQuest Dissertations and Theses Database. (UMI 3450260)

Darvish, H., & Rezaei, F. (2011). The impact of authentic leadership on job satisfaction and team commitment. *Management & Marketing,* 6(3), 421-436.

Dennis, R. S. (2004). *Servant leadership theory: Development of the servant leadership assessment instrument* (Doctoral dissertation). Available from ProQuest Dissertations and Theses database. (UMI 3133544)

Fry, L. W. (2003). Toward a theory of spiritual leadership. *The Leadership Quarterly,* (14), 693-727. doi:10.1016/j.leaqua.2003.09.001

George, D., & Mallery, P. (2010). *SPSS for Windows* (10th Ed.). Boston, MA: Allyn and Bacon.

Greenleaf, R. K. (1970). *The servant as leader.* Cambridge, MA: Center for Applied Studies.

Greenleaf, R. K. (1977). *Servant leadership: A journey into the nature of legitimate power and greatness.* Mahwah, NJ: Paulist Press.

Greenleaf, R. K. (2008). *The servant as leader* (Rev. Ed.). Westfield, IN: Greenleaf Center.

Greenleaf, R. K. (2009). *The institution as Servant* (Rev. Ed.). Westfield, IN: Greenleaf Center.

Hoveida, R., & Salari, S. (2011). A study on the relationship of servant leadership (SL) and the organizational commitment (CL): A case study. *Interdisciplinary Journal of Contemporary Research in Business, 3*(3), 499-509.

Joseph, E. E., & Winston, B.C. (2005). A correlation of servant leadership, leader trust, and organizational trust. *Leadership and Organization Development Journal, 26*(1), 6-22. doi: 10.1108/01437730510575552

Kouzes, J. M., & Posner, B. Z. (2004). *Christian reflections on Leadership Challenge.* San Francisco, CA: Jossey-Bass.

Kouzes, J. M. & Posner, B. Z. (2007). *The leader-ship challenge* (4th Ed.). San Francisco, CA: Jossey-Bass.

Kouzes, J. M., & Posner, B. Z. (2013a). *LPI: Leadership practices inventory: Facilitator's guide* (4th Ed.). San Francisco, CA: Pfeiffer.

Kouzes, J. M., & Posner, B. Z. (2013b). *LPI: Leadership practices inventory: Self* (4th Ed.). San Francisco, CA: Pfeffer.

McGrath-Merkle, C. (2010). Generativity and the U.S. Roman Catholic bishops' responses to priests' sexual abuse of minors. *Journal of Religious Health, 49,* 73- 86. doi: 10.1007/s10943-009-9288-0

Patterson, K. A. (2003). *Servant leadership: A theoretical model* (Doctoral dissertation). Available from ProQuest Dissertations and Theses database. (UMI 3082719)

Peus, C., Wesche, J. S., Streicher, B., Braun, S., & Frey, D. (2012). Authentic leader-ship: An empirical test of its antecedents, consequences, and mediating mechanism. *Journal of Business Ethics, 107*(3), 331-348. doi: 10.1007/s 10551-011-0142-3

Reed, L. L., Vidaver -Cohen, D., & Colwell, S. R. (2011). A new scale to measure executive servant leadership: Development, analysis, and implications for research. *Journal of Business Ethics, 101,* 415-434. doi: 10.1007/ s10551-010- 0729-1

Robert K. Greenleaf Center for Servant Leadership. (n.d.a). *About us.* Retrieved from https:// www.greenleaf.org/about-us/

Robert K. Greenleaf Center for Servant Leadership. (n.d.b). *History.* Retrieved from https:// www.greenleaf.org/about-us/

Russell, R. F., & Stone, A. G. (2002). *A review of ser-vant leadership attributes: Develop a practi-cal model. Leadership and Organizational Development Journal, 23*(3), 145-157. doi: 10.1108/01437730210424084

Sanders, J. O. (2003). *Spiritual leadership responding to God's call*. Nashville, TN: Leadership and Adult Publishing.

Sarantopoulos, N. D. (2008). *The relationship between values and leadership styles of nonprofit leaders* (Doctoral dissertation). Available from ProQuest Dissertations and Theses database. (UMI 3348686)

Schyns, B., & Schilling, J. (2013). How bad are the effects of bad leaders? A meta- analysis of destructive leadership and its outcome. *The Leadership Quarterly*, (24), 138-158. Retrieved from http://dx.doi.org/10.1016/j.leaqua.2012.09.001

Seidel, A. (2003). *Charting a bold course: Training leaders for 21st-century ministry*. Chicago, IL: Moody Publishers.

Sendjaya, S., & Sarros, J. C. (2002). *Servant Leadership: Its origin, development, and application in organizations. Journal Leadership and Organizational Studies,* 9(2), 57-64.

Slaughter, Mike (2014) *Renegade Gospel-The Rebel Jesus,* Nashville, TN: Abingdon Press, (pg. 19).

Smith, C. (2005). Servant leadership: The leadership theory of Robert K. Greenleaf. *Info 640-Management of Info Organizations.* Retrieved from http://www.carolsmith.us/downloads/640greenleaf.pdf

Smith, B. N., Montagno, R. V., & Kuzmenko, T.N. (2004). *Transformational and servant leadership: Content and contextual comparisons. Journal of leadership Organizational Studies, 10*(4), 80-91.

Teaching Guide
for Six Sessions
"Leader to Servant Leader"

There will be six sessions, two sessions per week

- LPI Assessment was done at home (email results) or in class. Introduction with a purpose of study using mini-research statistics.

- Foundation of Leadership Profit and Faith-based organizations, 21st-century leadership needing resumption of Christian Educators with Teaching. Resumption of in-training sessions for Profit organizations. Leadership theory.

- Comparing different types of leaders

- Leadership traits with Pitfalls and Standards.

- Five Models and ten traits for servant leadership.

- Assessments results and final session with a scale of their assessment using the LPI. (*purchase an LPI)

Greenleaf's (2008) character traits involve leaders at any level of leadership and do not require entitlement, nor do Greenleaf's traits involve followers. The seven factors from Tannenbaum and Schmidt (1973) were designed to encompass both leaders and followers, but Greenleaf's (2008) character is applicable for characterizing servant leaders, not followers. Additionally, Greenleaf (2008) indicated no leadership level exists within the

* Kouzes, J. M., & Posner, B. Z. (2013b). *LPI: Leadership practices inventory: Self* (4th Ed.). San Francisco, CA: Pfieffer.)

list of the 10 traits. The identified traits can occur at any level of leadership or any level of involvement in decision-making with any leader.

In comparing the factors and traits of Tannenbaum and Schmidt (1973) and Greenleaf (2008), character traits are nonspecific. The traits identified by Greenleaf (2008) appear to provide the image of a genuine leader who makes a difference in the lives of others. Based on his identified character traits, Greenleaf (2008) implicated that servant leaders are different in their performance and outlook as leaders. In observing modern leaders, Greenleaf's character traits are relevant for leaders who are called servants in FBOs.